I'm Thankful For...

Are you enjoying this journal?

If so, *leave a review* because I'd love to hear about your experience. Also, your reviews help me improve future books for you to enjoy. Have a wonderful day!

www.UncleAmon.com

Day: _____   Date: ____/____/_____

Today, I am thankful for…

_____

_____

_____

_____

_____

_____

Great things that happened today…

_____

_____

_____

_____

_____

Day: _____   Date: ___/___/_____

Today, I am thankful for…

_____

_____

_____

_____

_____

_____

Great things that happened today…

_____

_____

_____

_____

_____

Day: _____   Date: _____/_____/_____

Today, I am thankful for…

_____

_____

_____

_____

_____

Great things that happened today…

_____

_____

_____

_____

_____

Day: _____   Date: ___ / ___ / _____

Today, I am thankful for…

_____

_____

_____

_____

_____

_____

Great things that happened today…

_____

_____

_____

_____

_____

Day: _____   Date: ___/___/_____

Today, I am thankful for…

_____

_____

_____

_____

_____

Great things that happened today…

_____

_____

_____

_____

_____

Day: _____   Date: ____/____/_____

Today, I am thankful for…

_____

_____

_____

_____

_____

_____

Great things that happened today…

_____

_____

_____

_____

_____

Day: _____   Date: ____ / ____ / _____

Today, I am thankful for…

Great things that happened today…

Day: _____   Date: ____/____/_____

Today, I am thankful for…

_____

_____

_____

_____

_____

Great things that happened today…

_____

_____

_____

_____

_____

_____

Day: _____   Date: ___ / ___ / _____

Today, I am thankful for…

_____

_____

_____

_____

_____

Great things that happened today…

_____

_____

_____

_____

_____

Day: _____ Date: ____/____/_____

Today, I am thankful for…

_____

_____

_____

_____

_____

_____

Great things that happened today…

_____

_____

_____

_____

_____

_____

Day: _____   Date: ____/____/_____

Today, I am thankful for…

_____

_____

_____

_____

_____

Great things that happened today…

_____

_____

_____

_____

_____

Day: _____   Date: ____/____/_____

Today, I am thankful for…

_____

_____

_____

_____

_____

_____

Great things that happened today…

_____

_____

_____

_____

_____

Day: _____   Date: ____/____/_____

Today, I am thankful for…

_____

_____

_____

_____

_____

Great things that happened today…

_____

_____

_____

_____

_____

Day: _____   Date: ____/____/_____

Today, I am thankful for…

_____

_____

_____

_____

_____

_____

Great things that happened today…

_____

_____

_____

_____

_____

Day: _____   Date: ____/____/_____

Today, I am thankful for…

_____

_____

_____

_____

_____

Great things that happened today…

_____

_____

_____

_____

_____

Day: _____   Date: ___/___/_____

Today, I am thankful for…

_____

_____

_____

_____

_____

_____

Great things that happened today…

_____

_____

_____

_____

_____

Day: _____   Date: ____/____/_____

Today, I am thankful for…

_____

_____

_____

_____

_____

Great things that happened today…

_____

_____

_____

_____

_____

Day: _____   Date: ___/___/_____

Today, I am thankful for…

_____

_____

_____

_____

_____

Great things that happened today…

_____

_____

_____

_____

_____

Day: _____   Date: ___/___/_____

Today, I am thankful for…

_____

_____

_____

_____

_____

_____

Great things that happened today…

_____

_____

_____

_____

_____

_____

Day: _____   Date: ___/___/_____

Today, I am thankful for…

_____

_____

_____

_____

_____

_____

Great things that happened today…

_____

_____

_____

_____

_____

Day: _____   Date: ___/___/_____

Today, I am thankful for…

_____

_____

_____

_____

_____

Great things that happened today…

_____

_____

_____

_____

_____

Day: _____   Date: ____/____/_____

Today, I am thankful for…

_____

_____

_____

_____

_____

_____

Great things that happened today…

_____

_____

_____

_____

_____

_____

Day: _____   Date: _____/_____/_____

Today, I am thankful for…

_____

_____

_____

_____

_____

Great things that happened today…

_____

_____

_____

_____

_____

Day: _____   Date: ____/____/_____

Today, I am thankful for…

_____

_____

_____

_____

_____

_____

_____

Great things that happened today…

_____

_____

_____

_____

_____

_____

Day: _____   Date: ____/____/_____

Today, I am thankful for…

_____

_____

_____

_____

_____

Great things that happened today…

_____

_____

_____

_____

Day: _____   Date: ___/___/_____

Today, I am thankful for…

_____

_____

_____

_____

_____

_____

Great things that happened today…

_____

_____

_____

_____

_____

Day: _____   Date: ____/____/_____

Today, I am thankful for…

_____

_____

_____

_____

_____

_____

Great things that happened today…

_____

_____

_____

_____

_____

Day: _____   Date: ____/____/_____

Today, I am thankful for…

_____

_____

_____

_____

_____

_____

Great things that happened today…

_____

_____

_____

_____

_____

Day: _____   Date: ____/____/_____

Today, I am thankful for…

_____

_____

_____

_____

_____

_____

Great things that happened today…

_____

_____

_____

_____

_____

Day: _____   Date: ____/____/_____

Today, I am thankful for…

_____

_____

_____

_____

_____

_____

Great things that happened today…

_____

_____

_____

_____

_____

_____

Day: _____   Date: ____/____/_____

Today, I am thankful for…

_____

_____

_____

_____

_____

Great things that happened today…

_____

_____

_____

_____

_____

Day: _____   Date: ____/____/_____

Today, I am thankful for…

_____

_____

_____

_____

_____

_____

Great things that happened today…

_____

_____

_____

_____

_____

Day: _____   Date: ____/____/_____

Today, I am thankful for…

_____

_____

_____

_____

_____

Great things that happened today…

_____

_____

_____

_____

_____

Day: _____   Date: ___/___/_____

Today, I am thankful for…

_____

_____

_____

_____

_____

_____

Great things that happened today…

_____

_____

_____

_____

_____

Day: _____   Date: ____/____/_____

Today, I am thankful for…

_____

_____

_____

_____

_____

Great things that happened today…

_____

_____

_____

_____

_____

Day: _____   Date: ____ / ____ / _____

Today, I am thankful for…

_____

_____

_____

_____

_____

Great things that happened today…

_____

_____

_____

_____

_____

Day: _____   Date: ____/____/_____

Today, I am thankful for…

_____

_____

_____

_____

_____

Great things that happened today…

_____

_____

_____

_____

_____

Day: _____   Date: ____/____/_____

Today, I am thankful for…

_____

_____

_____

_____

_____

_____

Great things that happened today…

_____

_____

_____

_____

_____

Day: _____   Date: ____/____/_____

Today, I am thankful for…

_____

_____

_____

_____

_____

Great things that happened today…

_____

_____

_____

_____

_____

Day: _____   Date: ____/____/_____

Today, I am thankful for…

_____

_____

_____

_____

_____

Great things that happened today…

_____

_____

_____

_____

Day: _____   Date: ____/____/_____

Today, I am thankful for…

_____

_____

_____

_____

Great things that happened today…

_____

_____

_____

_____

Day: _____   Date: ____/____/_____

Today, I am thankful for…

_____

_____

_____

_____

_____

_____

Great things that happened today…

_____

_____

_____

_____

_____

Day: _____   Date: ____/____/_____

Today, I am thankful for…

_____

_____

_____

_____

_____

Great things that happened today…

_____

_____

_____

_____

_____

Day: _____   Date: ___/___/_____

Today, I am thankful for...

_____

_____

_____

_____

_____

_____

Great things that happened today...

_____

_____

_____

_____

_____

Day: _____   Date: ____/____/_____

Today, I am thankful for…

_____

_____

_____

_____

_____

Great things that happened today…

_____

_____

_____

_____

_____

Day: _____   Date: ___/___/_____

Today, I am thankful for…

_____

_____

_____

_____

_____

Great things that happened today…

_____

_____

_____

_____

_____

Day: _____   Date: ____/____/_____

Today, I am thankful for...

_____

_____

_____

_____

_____

Great things that happened today...

_____

_____

_____

_____

_____

Day: _____   Date: ___/___/_____

Today, I am thankful for…

_____

_____

_____

_____

_____

_____

Great things that happened today…

_____

_____

_____

_____

_____

_____

Day: _____   Date: ___ / ___ / _____

Today, I am thankful for…

_____

_____

_____

_____

_____

Great things that happened today…

_____

_____

_____

_____

Day: _____   Date: ____/____/_____

Today, I am thankful for…

_____

_____

_____

_____

_____

_____

Great things that happened today…

_____

_____

_____

_____

_____

Day: _____   Date: ____/____/_____

Today, I am thankful for...

_____

_____

_____

_____

_____

_____

Great things that happened today...

_____

_____

_____

_____

_____

_____

Day: _____   Date: ____/____/_____

Today, I am thankful for…

_____

_____

_____

_____

_____

Great things that happened today…

_____

_____

_____

_____

_____

Day: _____   Date: ____/____/_____

Today, I am thankful for…

_____

_____

_____

_____

_____

_____

Great things that happened today…

_____

_____

_____

_____

_____

_____

Day: _____   Date: ____/____/_____

Today, I am thankful for…

_____

_____

_____

_____

_____

_____

Great things that happened today…

_____

_____

_____

_____

_____

Day: _____   Date: ____/____/_____

Today, I am thankful for…

_____

_____

_____

_____

_____

Great things that happened today…

_____

_____

_____

_____

_____

Day: _____   Date: ____/____/_____

Today, I am thankful for…

_____

_____

_____

_____

_____

_____

Great things that happened today…

_____

_____

_____

_____

_____

Day: _____   Date: ____/____/_____

Today, I am thankful for…

_____

_____

_____

_____

_____

_____

Great things that happened today…

_____

_____

_____

_____

_____

Day: _____   Date: ___/___/_____

Today, I am thankful for…

_____

_____

_____

_____

_____

_____

Great things that happened today…

_____

_____

_____

_____

_____

Day: _____   Date: ____/____/_____

Today, I am thankful for…

_____

_____

_____

_____

_____

Great things that happened today…

_____

_____

_____

_____

_____

Day: _____   Date: ____/____/_____

Today, I am thankful for…

_____

_____

_____

_____

_____

_____

Great things that happened today…

_____

_____

_____

_____

_____

Day: _____   Date: ____/____/_____

Today, I am thankful for...

_____

_____

_____

_____

_____

Great things that happened today...

_____

_____

_____

_____

_____

Day: _____   Date: ___/___/_____

Today, I am thankful for…

_____

_____

_____

_____

_____

Great things that happened today…

_____

_____

_____

_____

_____

Day: _____   Date: ____/____/_____

Today, I am thankful for…

_____

_____

_____

_____

_____

Great things that happened today…

_____

_____

_____

_____

_____

Day: _____   Date: ____/____/_____

Today, I am thankful for...

_____

_____

_____

_____

_____

_____

Great things that happened today...

_____

_____

_____

_____

_____

_____

Day: _____   Date: ____/____/_____

Today, I am thankful for…

_____

_____

_____

_____

_____

_____

Great things that happened today…

_____

_____

_____

_____

_____

Day: _____   Date: ____/____/_____

Today, I am thankful for…

_____

_____

_____

_____

_____

Great things that happened today…

_____

_____

_____

_____

_____

Day: _____   Date: ____ / ____ / _____

Today, I am thankful for…

_____

_____

_____

_____

_____

_____

Great things that happened today…

_____

_____

_____

_____

_____

Day: _____   Date: ____/____/_____

Today, I am thankful for…

_____

_____

_____

_____

_____

_____

Great things that happened today…

_____

_____

_____

_____

_____

Day: _____   Date: ____/____/_____

Today, I am thankful for…

_____

_____

_____

_____

_____

Great things that happened today…

_____

_____

_____

_____

_____

Day: _____   Date: ____/____/_____

Today, I am thankful for…

_____

_____

_____

_____

_____

_____

Great things that happened today…

_____

_____

_____

_____

_____

Day: _____   Date: ____/____/_____

Today, I am thankful for…

_____

_____

_____

_____

_____

Great things that happened today…

_____

_____

_____

_____

_____

Day: _____   Date: ____/____/_____

Today, I am thankful for…

_____

_____

_____

_____

_____

_____

Great things that happened today…

_____

_____

_____

_____

_____

_____

Day: _____   Date: ___ / ___ / _____

Today, I am thankful for…

_____

_____

_____

_____

_____

_____

Great things that happened today…

_____

_____

_____

_____

_____

Day: _____   Date: ____/____/_____

Today, I am thankful for…

_____

_____

_____

_____

_____

_____

Great things that happened today…

_____

_____

_____

_____

_____

_____

Day: _____   Date: ____/____/_____

Today, I am thankful for…

_____

_____

_____

_____

_____

_____

Great things that happened today…

_____

_____

_____

_____

_____

Day: _____   Date: ____ / ____ / _____

Today, I am thankful for…

_____

_____

_____

_____

_____

_____

Great things that happened today…

_____

_____

_____

_____

_____

_____

Day: _____   Date: ____/____/_____

Today, I am thankful for...

_____

_____

_____

_____

_____

Great things that happened today...

_____

_____

_____

_____

_____

Day: _____   Date: ___/___/_____

Today, I am thankful for…

_____

_____

_____

_____

_____

_____

Great things that happened today…

_____

_____

_____

_____

_____

Day: _____   Date: ____/____/_____

Today, I am thankful for…

_____

_____

_____

_____

_____

_____

Great things that happened today…

_____

_____

_____

_____

_____

Day: _____   Date: ____/____/_____

Today, I am thankful for…

_____

_____

_____

_____

_____

_____

Great things that happened today…

_____

_____

_____

_____

_____

_____

Day: _____ Date: ___ / ___ / _____

Today, I am thankful for…

_____

_____

_____

_____

_____

_____

Great things that happened today…

_____

_____

_____

_____

_____

Day: _____   Date: ____/____/_____

Today, I am thankful for…

_____

_____

_____

_____

_____

Great things that happened today…

_____

_____

_____

_____

_____

Day: _____ Date: ___ / ___ / _____

Today, I am thankful for…

_____

_____

_____

_____

_____

Great things that happened today…

_____

_____

_____

_____

_____

Day: _____   Date: ____/____/_____

Today, I am thankful for…

_____

_____

_____

_____

_____

_____

Great things that happened today…

_____

_____

_____

_____

_____

Day: _____   Date: ____/____/_____

Today, I am thankful for…

_____

_____

_____

_____

_____

Great things that happened today…

_____

_____

_____

_____

_____

Day: _____   Date: ___/___/_____

Today, I am thankful for…

_____

_____

_____

_____

_____

_____

Great things that happened today…

_____

_____

_____

_____

_____

Day: _____   Date: _____ / _____ / _____

Today, I am thankful for…

_____

_____

_____

_____

_____

_____

Great things that happened today…

_____

_____

_____

_____

_____

Day: _____ Date: ____/____/_____

Today, I am thankful for…

_____

_____

_____

_____

_____

Great things that happened today…

_____

_____

_____

_____

_____

Day: _____   Date: ____/____/_____

Today, I am thankful for…

_____

_____

_____

_____

_____

_____

Great things that happened today…

_____

_____

_____

_____

_____

Day: _____   Date: ____/____/_____

Today, I am thankful for…

_____

_____

_____

_____

_____

_____

Great things that happened today…

_____

_____

_____

_____

_____

Day: _____   Date: ___/___/_____

Today, I am thankful for...

_____

_____

_____

_____

_____

Great things that happened today...

_____

_____

_____

_____

_____

Day: _____   Date: ____/____/_____

Today, I am thankful for…

_____

_____

_____

_____

_____

Great things that happened today…

_____

_____

_____

_____

_____

Day: _____   Date: ____ / ____ / _____

Today, I am thankful for…

_____

_____

_____

_____

_____

Great things that happened today…

_____

_____

_____

_____

_____

Day: _____   Date: ____/____/_____

Today, I am thankful for…

_____

_____

_____

_____

_____

_____

Great things that happened today…

_____

_____

_____

_____

_____

_____

Day: _____   Date: ____/____/_____

Today, I am thankful for…

_____

_____

_____

_____

_____

Great things that happened today…

_____

_____

_____

_____

_____

Day: _____   Date: ____/____/_____

Today, I am thankful for...

_____

_____

_____

_____

_____

_____

Great things that happened today...

_____

_____

_____

_____

_____

_____

Day: _____   Date: ____/____/_____

Today, I am thankful for…

_____

_____

_____

_____

_____

Great things that happened today…

_____

_____

_____

_____

_____

Day: _____   Date: ____/____/_____

Today, I am thankful for…

_____

_____

_____

_____

_____

_____

Great things that happened today…

_____

_____

_____

_____

_____

_____

Day: _____   Date: ____/____/_____

Today, I am thankful for...

_____

_____

_____

_____

_____

Great things that happened today...

_____

_____

_____

_____

_____

Day: _____ Date: ___/___/_____

Today, I am thankful for…

_____

_____

_____

_____

_____

_____

Great things that happened today…

_____

_____

_____

_____

_____

63040656R00057

Made in the USA
Middletown, DE
27 January 2018